Vegan Recipes from the Heart

Delicious eating for a meat-free, egg-free, dairy-free and nut-free family

Edy Henderson

AuthorHouse™
1663 Liberty Drive
Bloomington, IN 47403
www.authorhouse.com
Phone: 1-800-839-8640

First published by AuthorHouse 3/23/2010

ISBN: 978-1-4490-5400-7 (sc)

Library of Congress Control Number: 2009914343

Printed in the United States of America
Bloomington, Indiana

This book is printed on acid-free paper.

authorHOUSE®

I dedicate this book to my daughter Marlene who, because of her love for animals, decided early in life that it was not nice to eat animals.

Table of Contents

Side Dishes

Desserts

Introduction

This is a very personal collection of recipes developed and adapted over the years by and for our family to accommodate a history of special dietary needs.

My mother was a good cook, and her mother who was born in England shared recipes with her. Many of the recipes are inspired from family recipes that were passed down from relatives and friends. Our family also enjoys travel and I have added some international flavors.

Here is some history of when and how my daughter stopped eating meat. When my daughter was 2 ½, she looked at the sardines on her lunch plate, climbed down from her chair, walked over to look at the fish tank, climbed back up into her chair and said, "I'm not hungry."

At four she asked what was on her dinner plate. When I told her it was pork chops, she asked, "Exactly where do pork chops come from?"

Our neighbors went hunting and brought home a deer, hanging it in their garage to season it. She came running home yelling, "There's a real live 'begiraff' in the garage next door." After she was invited to dinner she came home saying that the steak tasted funny and that she thought they were eating Bambi.

Marlene still ate bar-b-q ribs, ground meat and shrimp until she was 11. Then she stopped eating meat and fish altogether. She loved animals and decided it was not nice to eat them. Well-meaning friends and relatives informed me that her diet would stunt her growth. I did some research and learned about combining foods such as grains and legumes to create complete proteins. I also met people from India at work who were vegetarians, and so I knew that it was possible to be healthy and vegetarian. When she graduated from High School, Marlene was 6'3" tall, was the starting center on her basketball team and had earned a full ride college basketball scholarship. I no longer worried about stunting her growth.

My own personal battle with health issues caused me to get in touch with my body. I learned that the American Cancer Society and the American Heart Association both recommend large amounts of fruits and vegetables as part of a low fat diet. I tried eliminating meat and felt much better, so I have stuck with a vegetarian diet for many years now.

In addition to being compassionate and healthy, a vegetarian diet is also "green". It takes a lot less water and energy to grow vegetables than it does to grow animals for food.

Marlene later decided to become vegan. In the meantime, my grandson developed a severe nut allergy. Many vegetarian cookbooks contain dairy products and many vegan cookbooks use nuts. These recipes contain no animal products and no nuts. We use soy, and food combinations to form complete proteins.

We use mostly complex carbohydrates. However, you have to have a few sweet treats sometimes, right? So we do include some delicious vegan desserts that contain simple carbohydrates.

In all, I think we have some very delicious and healthy recipes, and we hope you enjoy them as much as our family does.

By the way, these recipes get rave reviews from many family and friends who are non vegetarians, simply because they are delicious!

Enjoy! Bon appetite! Buen provecho!

Edy Henderson

Acknowledgements

I would like to thank my husband Joe for tasting and giving his feedback on these dishes even though he is neither vegan nor vegetarian. Also, I thank him for his patience waiting until photos had been taken before sitting down to eat.

I thank my daughter Marlene for contributing many of these recipes and for testing the recipes I developed.

Thank you to Alonzo and Joseph, Marlene's amazing sons who have given their candid opinions of my cooking, and who both enjoy helping out in the kitchen.

Thank you to my late mother Grace, her mother Bella, and my aunts for their wonderful recipes that have inspired adaptations for this book.

Thank you to friends who have shared recipes and given support and feedback: Pogie Calderon, Doreen Rovetti, Charla Rotter, my sister Patty Lockett and my cousin Nancy Neider LaRocque.

Appetizers

A few suggestions are included here as an alternate to the usual appetizers one finds at social events. Vegetable trays with olive oil and balsamic vinegar dressings are always welcome treats for the vegan. Many stores now offer olive bars with a variety of flavors. Hummus made from garbanzo beans comes in a variety of seasoned flavors, and serves as a good party dip, as does guacamole.

1 large fresh Artichoke   1 t Salt

1 t Olive Oil   3 T Nayonaise (Vegan Mayonaise substitute)

Cut stem off artichoke. Fill a large sauce pan with water, add oil, salt and artichoke and bring to a boil. Cover, reduce heat and simmer ~40 minutes until artichoke heart is soft when poked with a fork. May be served chilled. Serve with Nayonaise or melted vegan margarine for dipping.

Guacamole

2 ripe Avocados

½ Lime or Lemon

1 ripe Tomato: peeled, seeded, diced

½ t Seasoning Salt

Peel avocados, remove seed and place in a medium bowl. Using a pastry blender or fork, mash the avocados. Squeeze in the juice of ½ lime or lemon. Add diced tomato. Add seasoning salt and mix evenly. Serve immediately.

Use as a garnish or as a dip for vegetable sticks or chips.

Stuffed Mushrooms

12 Button Mushrooms

6 Saltine Crackers

1 clove Garlic

2 T Vegan Mozzarella Cheese alternative

2 T Red Wine

3 T Olive Oil

½ t Sesame Oil

1 t chopped Chives

½ t dried Cilantro

½ t Sage

½ t Salt

Heat oven to 350 degrees F.

Wipe mushrooms clean with a damp cloth. Remove stems. Place mushrooms cap side down in a baking pan. Chop stems finely in small bowl. Crush saltine crackers to make crumbs and add. Mince garlic, grate cheese alternative and add to stems. Add remaining ingredients and mix thoroughly.

Spoon the mixture into the mushroom caps. Bake for 20 minutes.

Cornbread Stuffed Mushrooms

24 button Mushrooms

1 medium Onion

2 Bell Peppers

5 stalks of Celery

1/4 cup Olive Oil

1 c Water or Vegetable Broth

Corn Bread (see Vegan Corn Bread Recipe)

1 t Sage

1 t Poultry Seasoning

1/2 t Salt

1/4 t Pepper

Heat oven to 350 degrees F.

Remove the stems from the mushrooms. Chop mushroom stems, onions, bell pepper, and celery.

Heat olive oil in a heavy skillet. Sauté onions, celery, bell pepper and mushrooms until soft. Stir in seasonings. Add liquid. Crumble in corn bread and stir in.

Place mushrooms on a cookie sheet. Spoon dressing into the mushrooms.

Bake for 30 minutes.

Deep Fried Zucchini Blossoms

1 ½ c all purpose Flour

2 c Beer

½ c cold Water

2 t fine sea Salt

3 Ice cubes

Extra virgin Olive Oil

Zucchini or nasturtium blossoms

Warm sea-salted Water in a sprayer

In a large bowl, beat together the flour, beer, water, and salt with a fork. Cover and let stand for one hour at room temperature. Stir in the ice cubes, re-cover and let stand for an additional half hour. Stir the batter. It should be the texture of heavy cream. If it is too thick, stir in cold water until the texture of heavy cream.

Slowly heat 3" of oil in a deep fryer over medium heat. Test the oil by dropping in a cube of bread. If it sizzles and turns golden in a few seconds it is ready.

Dip the flowers in the batter one at a time, and shake off excess batter. Place into the hot oil and let them bob for half a minute. When they develop a dark crust, turn with tongs to cook the other side. Remove with a slotted spoon onto absorbent paper towels.

Using a new plant sprayer, spray each batch immediately with warm sea-salted water and place in a 100-degree oven while frying the next batch. Serve immediately.

Soups

There is nothing more welcome than a hot bowl of soup on a cold winter day. Soup can be seasoned with vegetable stock, vegan bouillon cubes, herbs and spices. The soups included here are delicious and beautiful, a feast for the eyes as well as the palate.

Butternut Squash Soup

1 large Butternut Squash

1 medium sized Yam

1 medium sized Potato

1 large sweet Onion

1 ear of sweet Corn

2 T Olive Oil

2-3 cups Vegetable Stock

Heat oven to 350 degrees F.

Cut squash in half, brush cut side with olive oil and place face down on a baking dish. Bake squash and yam for 1 hour.

Boil potato until soft. Dice the onion. Slice the corn off the cob.

Sauté onion in 1 T olive oil for 5 minutes. Add sweet corn and sauté for another 10 minutes.

Cool squash and peel. Peel yam and potato. Puree squash, yam, and potato in a blender with vegetable stock.

Pour into a large sauce pan, add onion and corn and add additional vegetable stock to desired consistency. Serves 8.

Mushroom Barley Soup

3 cups Barley

¼ c Olive Oil

½ Onion

1 thinly sliced Carrot

6 cloves Garlic

3 cups chopped Mushrooms

¼ cup Braggs Liquid Amino

1 tsp Salt

½ tsp Pepper

½ tsp Cayenne Pepper

6 cups Water

Soak barley overnight. Rinse barley, cover with water in a sauce pan, bring to a boil, reduce heat, and simmer for 2 hours until soft.

In a heavy saucepan, heat olive oil. Add sliced onion, sliced carrot, minced garlic and chopped mushrooms. Stir and sauté until vegetables are soft. Add Braggs Liquid Amino seasonings, and water. Stir, heat to boiling, and simmer for 10-15 minutes. Serve warm with bread.

Serves 6 as an appetizer or serves 4 as a main course meal.

Minestrone Soup

2 T Olive Oil

1 medium Onion

1 large Carrot

2 cloves Garlic, minced

1 Zucchini Squash

1 yellow Crookneck Squash

6 Roma (or 1-14 oz. can) Tomatoes

½ lb fresh Spinach

1 T Oregano

1 T chopped Parsley

1 t Salt

4 c Vegetable Broth

1 can Garbanzo Beans

1 c whole kernel Corn

1 c cooked Pasta

Heat olive oil in a Dutch oven. Dice onion and sauté in oil until transparent. Remove from pan. Sauté sliced carrot until soft. Stir in minced garlic, sliced zucchini, sliced yellow crookneck squash, tomatoes, and spinach. Stir in oregano, parsley, salt, vegetable broth and onions. Cover and bring to a boil. Lower heat and simmer for 20 minutes, stirring occasionally. Carefully stir in beans, corn and cooked pasta. Heat for 5 minutes. Serves 8.

Minestrone Soup, Rice Variation

1 T Olive Oil	1/3 c Green Peas
½ Medium Yellow Onion	1 Quart Water
2 Carrot Sticks	1 ½ t Salt
1 Celery Stick	1 t Oregano
1/3 head of Broccoli	½ t Dash seasoning
1 clove Garlic	½ t Hot Sauce
¼ c shredded Cabbage	1/3 c Cooked Lentils
	1 c Cooked Rice

Heat olive oil in heavy skillet over medium heat. Dice onion and add to oil. Peel and slice carrots. Add to skillet, stirring well. Slice celery and cut broccoli and add, stirring well. Mince garlic and stir in along with cabbage and peas. Add water and turn heat up to high until water boils. Add salt, oregano, dash and hot sauce. Cover, reduce heat to medium and simmer for 5 minutes. Add lentils and rice and heat until boiling.

Serves 4.

Vegan Pumpkin Soup

1 medium Pumpkin or 1 can Pumpkin

1 quart Soy Milk

1 t Salt

½ t Cinnamon

¼ t Nutmeg

¼ t Ginger

½ t Parsley Flakes

Cut top off pumpkin and remove pulp. Cut into 2" square pieces and bake or boil until tender. Remove peel from pumpkin. (Alternatively you may substitute a can of precooked pumpkin).

Puree pumpkin and soy milk in a food processor or blender until liquefied.

Add, salt, cinnamon and nutmeg.
When ready to serve heat over medium burner and ladle into bowls. Garnish with parsley flakes.
Serves 4-6.

Salads

Salads are one of the easiest vegan foods to prepare. Just use your imagination and slice vegetables or fruit and dress with oil and vinegar or other dressing that contains no dairy. Some easy and attractive suggested combinations are: sliced tomatoes with cucumbers and basil or sliced kiwi with sliced pink grapefruit.

Some commercial salad dressings are vegan, so read the label carefully to avoid dairy and eggs. You can easily make your own dressings by combining oil, vinegar and or lemon/lime juice with seasonings such as garlic, cilantro, basil or other herbs, salt and pepper. Using a blender to combine herbs such as cilantro with the oil and vinegar can result in a beautiful green dressing.

Always wait until the last minute to add salt or dressings containing salt so that your salad vegetables will remain crisp.

Vegan Greek Salad

Dressing
¾ c Extra Virgin Olive Oil
2 T Lemon Juice
2 T Balsamic Vinegar
1 clove minced Garlic
½ t Salt
1/8 t freshly ground Pepper
1 T capers (optional)

Salad
8 crisp lettuce leaves
2 oz Firm Tofu
1/2 t Salt
2 T White Rice Vinegar
1 Sliced cucumber
¼ Sliced Red Spanish Onion
¾ t Oregano
¾ t Basil
4 Quartered Roma Tomatoes
Kalamata Olives

Slice tofu on a plate, sprinkle with salt, press by covering with another plate and placing a cup on top of the plate. Let stand for an hour. Drain tofu. Crumble tofu into a small bowl and sprinkle with rice vinegar and ¼ t salt. Set aside.

In a jar, add dressing ingredients, cover and shake well.

Tear crisp cold lettuce into bit sized pieces in a salad bowl. Peel cucumber, score outside with a fork, and slice into salad bowl. Add slice red onion, oregano and basil, and toss.
Add tomatoes and olives. Drain tofu and add. Sprinkle with dressing and toss again lightly.

Vegan Caesar Salad

1 clove Garlic, minced

2/3 c Extra Virgin Olive Oil

1 c cubed French bread

2 Heads Romaine Lettuce

¼ t Salt

¼ t Mustard

1 T Nayonaise (vegan Mayonaise)

½ t Soy Sauce

Juice of 1 Lemon

Add minced garlic to olive oil and let stand overnight.

Sauté 1 c cubed French bread in 2 T of garlic oil to make Croutons.

Wash and dry 2 heads of chilled Romaine lettuce.

Cut lettuce into 2" lengths into a salad bowl.

Add remaining ingredients to the rest of the oil. Whip with a wire whisk until smooth.

Add croutons to the salad.

Add dressing. Toss and serve immediately. Sprinkle with fresh ground pepper.

Cole Slaw

¼ head green Cabbage (chilled)   1 Lemon

3 medium Carrots (chilled)   ¼ c Nayonaise (Vegan mayonnaise substitute)

Shred green cabbage.

Grate carrots.

Add cabbage and carrots to a salad bowl and stir until well mixed. (This much can be prepared ahead of time.)

Squeeze lemon. Add the juice, stirring well.

Add 1/4 cup Nayonaise (Vegan mayonnaise) and stir until the vegetables are coated.

Mix and serve immediately.

Vegan Potato Salad

12 medium red Potatoes

2 T Olive Oil

20 Green pimento stuffed Olives

½ Green Bell Pepper

3 stalks Celery

4 slices Dill Pickles

1 tsp Mustard

1/3 c Nayonaise (Vegan mayonnaise)

1 T Cilantro or Parsley

½ t Paprika

1 t Salt

Boil potatoes with skins on until soft but still firm. Refrigerate.
Cut stuffed olives in half. Chop bell pepper and celery into small pieces (1/4"). Cut pickles into small pieces.

Slice potatoes and cut into ½" pieces. Pour olive oil evenly over potatoes. Add chopped vegetables, mustard, Nayonaise, cilantro, paprika and salt. Stir gently mixing well.
Place into a serving bowl and sprinkle paprika over the top. Serve chilled.

Main Dishes

Main dishes can be difficult to find for those who choose a diet free of meat, eggs, dairy and nuts. The basic ingredients for vegan main dishes include bean and grain based foods. Tofu, or soya bean paste, has become widely available everywhere, and provides an excellent source of proteins. Combining legumes and grains at the same meal is also a good way to provide complete proteins.

Many of the recipes in this section have been adapted from traditional recipes, and many are inspired by travel to Asia, the Mediterranean and Latin America.

Butternut Squash with Mushrooms and Tofu

1 medium sized Butternut Squash	3 T Canola Oil
10 oz. Dried Wood Ear Mushrooms	1 t ground Ginger
½ package firm Tofu	1 clove Garlic, minced
2 T Canola Oil	2 T Soy Sauce
6 Green Onions	2/3 c Water
	1 ½ t Corn Starch

Heat oven to 425 degrees. Bake squash until soft when pricked with a fork (~45 minutes)

Soak dried mushrooms in water for 30 minutes to reconstitute.

Cut tofu into ¼" by 1" strips. Press tofu by placing under a weighted plate for 30 minutes. Drain off excess water.

Mix sauce ingredients and stir over medium heat until thickened.

Cut green onions in to 1 ½" strips. Sauté in 2 T oil until soft. Remove set aside.

Sauté mushrooms in remaining oil.

Peel squash and cut into 1" cubes.

Gently mix squash, mushrooms, sauce, green onions and tofu until all ingredients are covered with sauce.

Serve with sticky Japanese rice.

2 T vegetable Oil

¼ Onion, sliced

½ c Broccoli

½ c baby Carrots

½ c Celery sliced diagonally

¼ c Cauliflower

1 c Spinach leaves

1 c Snow Peas

1 t powdered Ginger

2 T Soy Sauce

8 oz. firm Tofu

In wok or skillet, heat vegetable oil. Stir in onion, broccoli, carrots, celery and cauliflower. Continue stirring on high heat for 5 minutes. Stir in spinach and snow peas. Sprinkle ginger over mixture, add soy sauce, and stir until thoroughly mixed. Add cubed tofu. Cover pan, reduce heat to low and cook for 5 minutes more. This is good served with pasta or rice.

Vegan Chile Verde

14 oz Firm Tofu

2 T Soy Sauce

4 T Olive Oil

1 medium white Onion chopped

3 cloves Garlic

1/3 cup Flour

½ pound button Mushrooms

2-6" Anaheim chili peppers

8 Jalapeno chili peppers

12 Tomatillos

1 quart Water

1 t Salt

1/2 t Oregano

Cut tofu into 1/2" cubes. Marinate tofu in soy sauce for 10 minutes.

Heat 2 T olive oil in a heavy frying pan, add chopped onion and sauté until transparent. Add minced garlic. Sauté until onion is light brown. Remove onions and garlic and set aside. Slice mushrooms and brown in the frying pan. Remove and set aside. Dice chili peppers, add to frying pan and sauté until soft. Remove.

Heat 2 T olive oil in frying pan. Brown tofu on all sides. Remove and set aside.

Add flour to frying pan and stir constantly until brown. Stir in water mixing with a wire whisk until smooth. (If lumps form, put gravy in blender and liquefy, then return to frying pan). Add cooked onions, garlic, salt, mushrooms and oregano. Remove "paper lantern" outside from tomatillos, cut into small pieces and add.

Bring to a boil. Reduce heat and simmer for 20 minutes stirring occasionally.
Stir in tofu and mushrooms and simmer for 5 more minutes.
Serve with steamed rice and warm tortillas. Serves 4-6.

Enchiladas

This is an adaptation of an old family recipe that my mother learned from a neighbor. The original recipe called for cheese, hardboiled eggs and tortillas made with lard.

It is a family tradition to fill the enchiladas "assembly line" style with the fillings prepared ahead of time.

After a tortilla is dipped in sauce, the pan can be passed down the "assembly line" for each person to add a filling. Fold and cover with cheese and sauce before baking.

Filling:	Sauce:	1 dozen flour Tortillas (read
½ c Water	3 T Olive Oil	label to made sure they
1 large white Onion	3 T Flour	contain only vegetable oil)
1-14 oz package Soft Tofu	1-28 oz can Las Palmas	
1-11 oz can whole Corn	enchilada sauce	
2-12 oz packages Soya	2 T Oregano	
cheese, Cheddar style	1 t. Salt	
1 can pitted black Olives	1 can Water	
	2 cloves minced Garlic	

Prepare Filling:

Dice onion, and simmer in water 15 minutes. Crumble tofu in a bowl. Grate cheese and place in another bowl. Open olives and corn.

Prepare Sauce:
Heat olive oil in a large skillet. Add flour, and stir until smooth and bubbly. Slowly stir in enchilada sauce, oregano, salt, and water and garlic. Simmer for 20 minutes, stirring often.
Oil two large baking pans. Dip a tortilla in skillet to cover with sauce. Place tortilla in a baking pan. Fill tortilla with a large spoonful of tofu, onion, corn, 3 olives, and cheese. Fold tortilla to close enchilada. Top with grated cheese and sauce. Bake at 350 for 20 minutes. Makes 1 dozen.

Fall Stew

2 T Olive Oil

½ White Onion

½ medium Butternut Squash

2 Red Pimento Peppers

1 Green Pimento Pepper

2 Red Fresno Chili Peppers

1 Zucchini Squash

1 clove Garlic, minced

1 T Soy Sauce

3 T Water

¼ c Fresh Basil Leaves

Cut the onion, squash and pimentos into cubes. Slice the Fresno chili in thin strips.
Heat olive oil in a skillet over medium heat. Add onion and butternut squash and sauté for 5 minutes, stirring often. Add all the peppers and stir another 5 minutes. Stir in the minced garlic. Add soy sauce and water and stir in the fresh basil leaves. Turn heat to low, cover and cook for 5 minutes more.

Serve with rice.

Curried Cauliflower Sauté

Gravy:
1 T Curry Powder
1 t Powdered Ginger
1 t Oregano
½ t Salt
¼ c Red Wine
1 T Vegetable Oil
1 T Water

2 T Vegetable Oil
½ Diced Purple Onion
12 Sliced Button Mushrooms
½ Cauliflower
¼ c Garbanzo Beams
4 oz cubed Tofu

In a small bowl, mix curry powder, ginger, oregano, salt wine, oil and water to make gravy. Set aside.

In skillet, heat oil over medium heat, add diced onion, and stir. Stir in sliced mushrooms.
Cut cauliflower into small flowers and add. Stir, cooking for five minutes. Stir in garbanzo beans and tofu. Add gravy, cover, and turn heat to low and let cook for 7 minutes.

Rice	Mushrooms	Broccoli
1 ¾ C water	2 T Olive Oil	1 head of Broccoli
½ t Salt	½ lb Maitake Mushrooms	2 T Water
1 c Chinese Forbidden Rice		2 T vegan Margarine

In a saucepan, add 1¾ c water, ½ t salt, and 1 c Chinese Forbidden Rice.
Cover and bring to a boil, reduce heat and simmer for 30 minutes.

In a frying pan, heat 2T olive oil, add Maitake mushrooms, stir and sauté for 2 minutes, cover and simmer another 5 minutes. Add 1 T soy sauce and stir.

Steam broccoli in microwave for 5 minutes in covered container with 2 T water and 2 T vegan margarine. Serves 4. Total preparation time 35 minutes.

1 pound fresh Green Beans	½ pound Yellow Corn Kernels
2 T Vegan Margarine	1 T margarine
1 t Salt	½ t Paprika

Wash and cut the green beans. Steam until tender (7-10 minutes). Mix with 2 T Margarine and salt.

Sauté corn in 1 T margarine for 3 minutes.

Serve corn on top of green beans. Sprinkle with paprika.

This is listed under Main Dishes because combining corn and beans creates a complete protein.

Vegan Lasagna

16 oz Package Lasagna Noodles

6.5 oz Tofu-Veggie Burgers (2 patties)

25 oz jar Marinara Sauce

1 T Sweet Basil

½ t. Garlic Salt

½ t. Salt

2 c sliced Mushrooms

2 T Olive Oil

¼ c chopped Italian Parsley

1 c cooked Spinach

10 oz Mozzarella Style Soya Cheese

Heat oven to 350 degrees F. Boil noodles for 10 minutes. Cut veggie burgers into small pieces and brown over medium heat in a large skillet. Stir in and heat marinara sauce, sweet basil, garlic salt and salt. Set aside.

Slice mushrooms. Heat olive oil in a skillet, add mushrooms and cook 5 minutes over medium head. Stir in chopped parsley.

Oil the bottom of a 13" x 9" x 2" baking pan. Arrange 4 pasta strips lengthwise to cover bottom of pan. Spread a layer of spinach, then mushrooms and sauce. Top with sliced mozzarella style soya cheese. Add another layer of noodles. Repeat layering other ingredients. End with a layer of pasta, and cover with sauce mixture.

Cover pan with foil and back 55 minutes. Let stand 10 minutes before cutting. Serves 8.

Vegan Mushroom Risotto

4 Tbsp Margarine

2 cups Portabella Mushrooms

1/2 cup White Wine

3/4 cup Soy Milk

7 cups Vegetable Stock

1 Tbsp Extra-Virgin Olive Oil

6 Tbsp of yellow onion, finely chopped

1 3/4 cups Risotto rice

1 t Salt

ground Pepper to taste

2 Tbsp Oregano

Melt 2T margarine in a skillet over medium heat. Add mushrooms. Sauté 5 minutes. Add wine, bring to a boil, and boil 4 minutes. Lower heat to medium, stir in soy milk, and simmer 5 minutes. Remove from heat. Bring stock to a simmer in a saucepan.

Heat olive oil and 2T margarine in a deep, heavy medium sized skillet. Add onions and sauté until soft. Stir in rice. Add simmering stock, 1/2 cup at a time, stirring to keep the rice from sticking. When stock is almost absorbed, add another 1/2 cup until all the stock is used and the rice is done.
Stir in the mushroom mixture. Season to taste with salt and pepper and serve garnished with oregano. Serves 8 to 10.

Vegan Paella

2 c uncooked Rice

6 Roma Tomatoes, sliced

2 sliced sweet red Peppers

12 button Mushrooms

1 c green Peas

12 Artichoke Hearts

½ Bunch Italian Parsley

¼ c Olive Oil

½ Spanish Purple Onion

2 cloves Garlic

4 c Vegetable Broth

1-2 t Saffron

5 oz firm Tofu marinated in 2 T soy sauce

Preheat oven to 350 degrees. Use a casserole dish or skillet with a tight fitting cover.

In casserole dish, heat olive oil to moderate heat. Stir in diced onion and minced garlic. Dissolve saffron in the vegetable broth.

Stir rice into the casserole dish, then add broth and bring to a simmer. Add tomatoes, peppers, and mushrooms. Cover and bake at 350 degrees for 15 minutes. Add peas, artichoke hearts, parsley and tofu. Cover and steam 10 minutes longer until liquid is absorbed and rice is soft. Depending on the type of pan used, this may take longer. Serve immediately.

16 oz package of Bow Tie Pasta

3 T Extra Virgin Olive Oil

2 T Corn or Canola Oil

½ purple Onion

8 Button Mushrooms

½ Bell Pepper

½ c Broccoli

2 cloves minced Garlic

1 c Marinara Sauce

1 small jar marinated Artichoke Hearts

½ c canned Kidney Beans

2 dozen Pitted Kalamata Olives

4 oz. Sun Dried Tomatoes

1 T capers

12 Fresh Basil leaves

Boil pasta according to instructions on package. Drain. Gently stir olive oil into pasta.

Heat corn or canola oil in a frying pan.

Dice onion. Slice mushrooms and bell pepper into thin slices. Add to frying pan. Add broccoli.

Sauté 5 minutes in oil stirring constantly.

Mince garlic and add, then stir in marinara sauce, whole jar of artichoke hearts (un-drained), drained kidney beans, olives, sun dried tomatoes, capers, and basil. Heat to simmering. Combine with pasta.

Serve with garlic bread.

Rigatoni Arabiata

4 T Olive Oil	1 t Salt
1 medium Onion	1 t Fresh Oregano (or ½ t dried)
3 cloves minced Garlic	1 t chopped Parsley
1 Fresno Chili, finely chopped	1 T chopped Basil Leaves
6 Button Mushroom	15 fresh medium Tomatoes

In a large skillet, heat olive oil over medium heat. Stir in chopped onion, garlic, chili, and mushrooms. Saute over low heat.

Bring 3 cups of water to a boil in a saucepan. Dip tomatoes in boiling water. Remove tomatoes and slip off skins. Chop tomatoes and stir into skillet mixture. Add seasonings. Heat to boiling, reduce heat to low, and simmer for 2 hours.

Cook rigatoni according to instructions on package and cover with sauce.

12 oz package Fettuccini

3 T Extra Virgin Olive Oil

½ white Onion

6 Shitaki Mushrooms

4 c chopped Broccoli

2 cloves minced Garlic

¼ c grated vegan Parmesan style Cheese

1 small jar marinated Artichoke Hearts

2 dozen Pitted Kalamata Olives

1 t Capers

1 T dried Basil

1 t Jane's Krazy Mixed-up Salt

1 fresh Tomato

Boil pasta according to instructions on package. Drain.

Heat 1 T olive oil in a heavy skillet to medium high. Dice onion and add to skillet, stirring until golden brown. Remove and set aside. Cut broccoli into small pieces. Slice mushrooms. Add 2T olive oil to skillet. Add broccoli and mushrooms. Cook, stirring for 5 minutes. Mince 2 cloves of garlic and stir in, cooking for one more minute.

Gently stir cooked vegetables into pasta. Add parmesan cheese, artichoke hearts, olives, capers, basil, and seasoning salt to pasta. Gently stir until well mixed. Add diced peeled tomato. Serve with garlic bread. Serves 6-8.

Polenta with Portabella Mushroom

2 T Corn Oil	2 c Polenta
5 oz baby Spinach	4 Portabella Mushrooms
¼ t Salt	4 t Sesame Oil
4 roasted Red Peppers	4 small sprigs of fresh Rosemary

Heat oven to 400 degrees F. Remove stems from portabella mushrooms and carefully wipe clean with a damp paper towel. Rub 1 t. sesame oil into the top of each mushroom. Place mushrooms upside down on a baking dish. Bake 10 minutes. Turn mushrooms over and bake another 5 minutes.

Heat corn oil in a skillet over medium heat. Stir in fresh spinach. Sprinkle with salt and sauté stirring until spinach wilts. Remove from heat.

Heat polenta and red peppers in separate containers.

Arrange spinach on dinner plate, then top with roasted red pepper, then arrange polenta and top with a portabella mushroom and garnish with fresh rosemary. Serves 4.

Ratatouille

4 T Olive Oil

1 Medium Onion

2 Bell Peppers

1 Medium Eggplant

1 Medium Zuccini

4-5 Tomatoes

2 Cloves Garlic

½ tsp. Salt

Heat olive oil in a large skillet on medium heat. Stir in sliced onions, sliced peppers and sliced eggplant. Cook for 2 minutes. Add sliced squash. Add peeled, chopped tomatoes, and stir in minced garlic and salt. Cover, turn heat to low and simmer for 20 minutes. Serve over rice. Serves 4.

1 Package Rigatoni Pasta	3 Tbs Margarine
4 Cups Brussels Sprouts	Salt (to taste)
1/2 Red Onion	Pepper (optional)
1/2 Lemon (use juice only)	

Cook Rigatoni until al dente, set aside.
Microwave or steam 4 cups brussels sprouts for 2 - 3 minutes
Slice brussels sprouts in half.
Chop 1/2 red onion.
Melt margarine in skillet, medium heat. When melted, add brussels sprouts, and onions. Stirring constantly until slightly browned (about 10 minutes)
Add about 1/2 tsp. salt (or salt to taste). Drizzle lemon juice over brussels sprouts and mix with pasta.
Add salt and pepper to taste. Serves about 4 - 6 people.

Marinated Shish Kabobs with Wild Rice

1 Medium Sweet Spanish Onion

1 Large Zucchini

3 Large Portobello Mushrooms

14 Oz Firm Tofu

1 tsp. Salt

½ Cup Balsamic Vinaigrette

¼ Cup Agave Syrup

Cut onion, zucchini, mushrooms and tofu into 1" x 2" pieces. Place in a large bowl and sprinkle salt over all ingredients. Cover and let sit for 15 minutes. Dribble with balsamic vinaigrette. Cover and let sit again for 5 minutes. Dribble with agave syrup.

Alternate on each skewer onion, zucchini round, mushroom, and tofu.
Grill on barbeque turning frequently until vegetables are soft.
Place skewers on a platter. Serve next to or over wild rice pilaf.

Shish Kabob

12 White Pearl Onions
1 Zucchini
12 Button Mushrooms
½ Bell Pepper
1 Japanese Eggplant

1 clove Garlic
½ c Olive Oil
2 T Balsamic Vinegar
4" sprig of fresh Rosemary

Mince garlic and mix with olive oil and vinegar. Cut bell pepper into pieces approximately 1 ½" square. Cut zucchini and eggplant into ½" rounds. Alternate on each skewer: onion, zucchini round, mushroom, and bell pepper.

Dip rosemary sprig into oil mixture and use it to baste the vegetable skewers.

Grill on barbeque turning frequently until vegetables are soft.
Place skewers on a platter and salt lightly. Serve with brown rice.

Spaghetti Squash

1 Spaghetti Squash

1 cup chopped Tomato

1/3 cup sliced Green Onions

1 Tbsp. Lemon Juice

1 tsp. dried Basil

1 tsp. dried Oregano

4 tsp. Garlic Powder

Salt and Pepper to taste

Heat oven to 350 degrees F.

Cut squash in half. Place the squash, cut side down, on a greased cookie sheet. Bake about 30-45 minutes or until a knife pierces the skin without resistance. Allow the squash to cool and scoop out and discard the seeds. Using a fork, scrape the flesh into strands. In a Dutch oven or large pot, add tomatoes, green onions, lemon juice, basil, oregano, garlic salt, salt and pepper. Toss well to coat with sauce. Cook 1 minute over medium heat. Serves 6-8.

Stuffed Bell Peppers

4 fresh Bell or Pimento Peppers
2 T Olive Oil
1 small Onion
1 clove Garlic

1 medium Tomato
1 t fresh Basil
1 t fresh Chives
1 ½ cup cooked Rice

Preheat oven to 350 degrees.

Cut three bell peppers lengthwise and remove seeds. Chop remaining bell pepper.
Heat olive oil in skillet over medium heat. Add chopped onion, chopped pepper and minced garlic to oil, stirring often. Peel and chop tomato and add. Stir in basil and chives. Add cooked rice.

Fill bell peppers with mixture. Bake at 350 for 35 minutes. Serves 3-4.

Tostada

2 T Olive Oil

8 Corn Tortillas

1 Can Vegetarian Refried Beans

8 oz Soy Cheese

8 oz Salsa

4 Leaves Red Lettuce

1 Tomato cut into ½" pieces

½ Shredded Cabbage

1 Shredded Carrot

Vinaigrette Salad Dressing mixed with 1 oz Salsa

1 Avocado

24 Olives

Dried Red Chili Peppers

Toss the vegetables together with the salad dressing and 1 oz Salsa in a bowl.
Heat refried beans in a saucepan stirring until bubbly.
Heat tortillas one at a time in olive oil in a skillet, turning to heat both sizes.
Assemble each tostada on a separate plate:
Arrange 2 tortillas per plate, and spread refried beans on top. Sprinkle soy cheese on the beans, then spread 1 oz of salsa on top. Spoon the vegetables on top of the tostada. Add sliced avocado and olives. Sprinkle with dried red chili peppers to taste.
Serves 8. Serve immediately.

Tamales

I learned to make tamales from a friend who lived in Mexico for several years. Tamales are a family tradition for Christmas or New Years in many families. They can be made ahead of time and frozen in freezer bags, then steamed to defrost and reheat for serving.

It is a family tradition for people to gather together in the kitchen to assemble the tamales together.

Premixed Masa usually contains lard, so I mix my own and use olive oil instead.

Masa for Tamales:
2 c Masa Harina flour
1 t Salt
1 T Baking Powder
2 T Olive Oil
1 ½ c warm Vegetable Broth

In a large bowl, mix masa harina, salt and baking powder. Create a well at the top. Add olive oil and warm vegetable broth or water to the well. Mix thoroughly by hand until dough holds together but is not sticky.

12 Dried Corn Husks (hojas)	1 t Cumin
4 T Olive Oil	1 t Salt
1 Large Onion	2 T Oregano
12 Roma Tomatoes	1 bunch Italian Parsley
3 cloves Garlic	1 c vegetarian Refried Beans
2 8 oz. cans Tomato Sauce	1-14 oz package Soft Tofu
4 c Vegetable Broth	

Soak dried corn husks (hojas) in water for 30 minutes until pliable.

Heat olive oil in a Dutch Oven. Dice onions and tomatoes. Mince garlic. Add onions and sauté until lightly browned. Add tomatoes, garlic, tomato sauce, vegetable broth, cumin, salt, oregano, and Italian parsley. Stir well. Bring to a boil and cook over low heat for 45 minutes, uncovered. Reserve 2 cups of sauce and set aside for later.

Mash or puree refried beans. Crumble soft tofu. Add beans and tofu to sauce in Dutch oven, mixing thoroughly.

Place a 1" ball of masa on the inside of a cornhusk. Spread masa to form a rectangle in the middle, leaving the edges free. Fill the center of the masa with the filling, leaving sides free. Bring the sides together so that the masa sticks together on top, and wrap the cornhusk around the tamale. Steam tamales for 1½ hours. Serve with remaining sauce.

Side Dishes

No holiday feast is complete without an assortment of side dishes, breads and sauces. Here are some ideas that provide a complement to any meal. I always believe that food should be a feast for the eyes as well as the stomach.

Roasted Eggplant

4 T Olive Oil

1/4 c. Chopped Parsley

2 c Japanese Eggplant, sliced

4 Tbsp Fresh Basil

8 small Red Peppers, halved and seeded

½ t. salt

2 Heirloom Tomatoes

Preheat oven to 350 degrees F.

Drizzle a baking pan with 2 T olive oil. Slice eggplant, peppers and tomato. Arrange over olive oil and top with parsley, basil and salt. Drizzle the top with the remaining 2 T olive oil.

Cover baking pan and bake for 30 minutes.
Serve with rice, potatoes or pasta.

Serves 4.

Collard Greens

2 Bunches Collard Greens	½ t Salt
2 T Olive Oil	¼ t Baking Soda
½ Purple Onion	¼ c Water

Wash collard leaves thoroughly and cut into 2" strips. Do not dry.

Heat olive oil in a heavy skillet. Dice onion and sauté lightly in oil. Add collard greens to skillet, stirring in a little at a time. Sprinkle salt over greens and stir. Cover and reduce heat until greens cook down, being careful not to scorch them. If they become dry, add water 2 T at a time. Stir in baking soda. Cover and cook on low heat for 45 minutes to 1 hour, stirring often and checking to see if more water is needed.

Shown here served with baked yams and brown rice.

Collard greens tend to be tough and take a longer amount of cooking time than most greens.

1 Bunches Mustard Greens (about 20 leaves)
2 T Canola Oil
½ t Salt

Heat canola oil in a wok or heavy skillet over medium heat. Wash mustard leaves thoroughly and chop leaves into 2" strips. Do not dry. Add greens to skillet, stirring in a little at a time. Sprinkle salt over greens and stir. Cover, reduce heat to low and cook until greens cook down, being careful not to scorch them. If they become dry, add water 2 T at a time. Cover and cook on low heat for 20 minutes or until tender to the taste. Stir often and add more water if they become dry.

Mustard greens have a strong spicy flavor of their own so do not require additional seasoning.

Roasted Vegetables

1 head Broccoli

2 Carrots

1 Red Bell Pepper

½ Onion

12 Mushrooms

4 T Olive Oil

2 T Basil

½ t salt

Set broiler to 450 degrees F.

Peel carrots. Cut broccoli, carrots, bell peppers and onions into strips or bite sized pieces. Place on a large cookie sheet and drizzle with olive oil and basil.

Place under broiler and broil for 10 minutes. Turn vegetables and return to broiler for ~5 minutes, watching carefully until vegetables are soft and lightly browned, but not overcooked. Remove from broiler and sprinkle with salt.

Shown served with brown rice. Alternatively may be served as finger food with a dip. Serves 4.

Creamed Onions

2 pounds Boiling Onions
1 quart Water
2 T Vegan Margarine
1/2 t Salt

2 T White Flour
1 c Soya Milk
1 T Chives

Peel Onions. Bring water to a boil in a medium sauce pan. Boil onions until soft. Drain. (Liquid may be kept to use for soup or for vegetable broth).

In a double boiler, melt margarine. Stir in flour and salt with a wire whisk or a wooden spoon and continue to stir until bubbly. Slowly add soya milk, stirring constantly until smooth. Continue stirring until the sauce thickens. Place onions in a serving bowl, cover with sauce, and garnish with chives.

4 Medium Russet Potatoes

2 T White Flour

1 t Salt

¼ t Garlic Powder

¼ t. Paprika

5 T Vegan Margarine

2 T chopped Parsley

1 ¼ c Soy Milk

Heat oven to 350 degrees F.

Use 1 T margarine to grease a 10 inch square baking pan.

Place flour, salt, garlic powder, and paprika in a paper bag. Shake to mix.

Peel potatoes and slice into ¼ inch rounds. Add to paper bag and shake until potatoes are evenly coated. Arrange potatoes in layers in the baking pan, dotting with remaining margarine and parsley.

Heat soy milk over low heat until scalding. Pour milk over potatoes.

Cover and bake for ½ hour. Remove cover and continue to bake for 1 more hour.

Serves 4.

Sweet Potato Delight

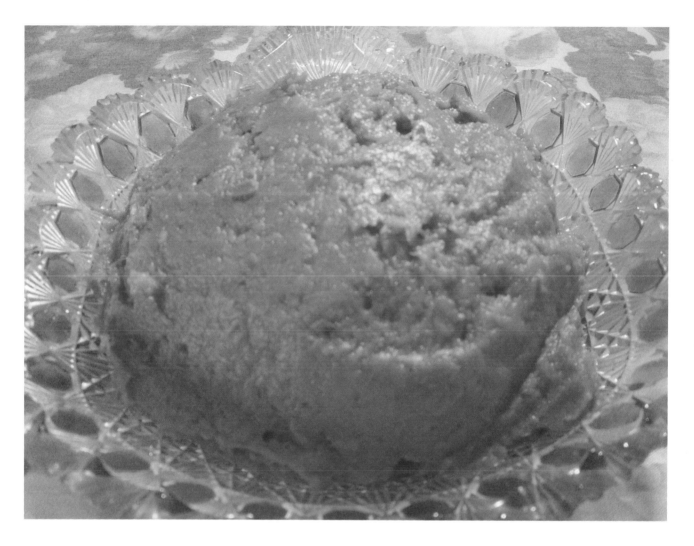

2 large Sweet Potatoes

1 medium Butternut Squash

1 tsp. Cinnamon

½ tsp. Ginger

¼ tsp. Nutmeg

¼ - ½ cup Soy Milk

Nutmeg for garnish

Heat oven to 375 degrees F.

Cut butternut squash into pieces approximately 4 inches square. Bake sweet potato and butternut squash 1 hour. Remove from oven and let stand until cool enough to handle. Peel squash and yam. Mash together or blend together in a food processor (a blender will not do the job) with spices. While processing, slowly add enough soy milk to make the consistency slightly looser than mashed potatoes. Place the mixture in an ovenproof dish, about 1 1/2 Qt. Sprinkle nutmeg on top as a garnish and bake at 350° for about 15 minutes. Serves 8.

Thanksgiving Stuffing

1 medium sized Pumpkin

1 medium Onion

2 Bell Peppers

5 stalks of Celery

1 cup chopped Mushrooms

1/4 cup Olive Oil

Corn Bread (see Vegan Corn Bread)

4 slices toasted Whole Wheat Bread

1 t Sage

1 t Poultry Seasoning

1/2 t Salt

1/4 t Pepper

1 c Water or Vegetable Broth

Cut the top off a medium size pumpkin. Remove seeds and pulp.

Chop onions, bell pepper, celery, and mushrooms.
Heat olive oil in a heavy skillet. Sauté onions, celery, bell pepper and mushrooms until soft. Stir in seasonings. Add 1 cup water or vegetable broth. Crumble in corn bread, break toast into small pieces and stir in. Place pumpkin on a cookie sheet. Stuff pumpkin with dressing. Bake for 40 minutes at 350 degrees. Carefully transfer pumpkin to a serving plate and it is ready to serve.

White Beans

4 cups Water
1 cup dried White Beans
4 cups Water
½ t Salt

1 T Olive Oil
2 cloves Garlic
1 sprig fresh Rosemary
1 t Sage

Soak beans in water overnight. Rinse beans. Place in a sauce pan with 4 cups more water, salt, olive oil, garlic and herbs. Simmer over low heat for 2-3 hours until beans are soft but still hold their shape.

Serve warm in soup bowls with bread or serve with brown rice for a complete protein.

This is a traditional dish in the Tuscan region of Italy.

1 Cup wild Rice

1 Tbsp. Vegan Margarine

2 Cubes Vegan Bouillon

½ tsp Salt

2 Cups Water

Bring water to a boil in a large saucepan. Add rice, margarine, bouillon and salt and stir once. Cover with a tight fitting lid. Bring to a boil again, then reduce heat to low and simmer for 50 minutes. Fluff with a fork before serving. Serves 4 to 6.

2 1/4 c tepid Water	6 1/2 cups all purpose Flour
1 scant tsp Brown Sugar	1 cup finely ground Cornmeal
1 T active dry Yeast	2 T fine Sea Salt
½ cup extra virgin Olive Oil	2 T fresh crushed Rosemary

Stir sugar and yeast into tepid water in a large mixing bowl. Let stand five minutes. Combine olive oil and 1 ½ T salt. Add to the yeast. Stir in flour a cup at a time. Stir in cornmeal. Turn onto a lightly floured surface and knead for 10 minutes. Add more water if too stiff to be workable, or add more flour if too sticky. Turn into a lightly oiled bowl, cover with plastic wrap, and let rise until double (one to two hours). Deflate the dough and cut into three pieces. Place onto oiled baking sheets which have been lightly sprinkled with cornmeal. Press with fingers to flatten. Cover with kitchen towels and let rise for 30 minutes. Press your knuckles into the dough, making little pockets. Cover again and let rise one more hour.

Pre-heat oven to 450 degrees F.

Sprinkle loaves with rosemary and sea salt. Drizzle with olive oil into the pockets. Back for 20-25 minutes until puffy and golden. Cool on wire racks.

Vegan Corn Bread

1 c yellow Corn Meal

1 c all-purpose Flour

¼ c Sugar

1 Tbsp Baking Powder

1 tsp Salt

1 ½ tsp ENER G Egg Replacer

2 Tbsp Water

1 cup Soy Milk

1/3 cup Vegetable Oil

Preheat oven to 400. Grease 8" square baking pan.

Mix dry ingredients in a mixing bowl.
In another small bowl mix egg replacer and water until dissolved.
Stir in soy milk and vegetable oil. Add to dry ingredients and stir until blended. Pour into baking pan.

Bake 20-25 minutes.

Zucchini Bread

1 cup all-purpose Flour

½ cup Whole Wheat Flour

¾ cup Sugar

¼ tsp Cinnamon

1 ½ tsp Baking Soda

½ tsp Salt

1 Tbsp ENER G Egg Replacer

¼ cup Water

1 tsp Vanilla

½ cup Vegetable Oil

1 ½ cups grated Zucchini

Preheat oven to 350. Grease a bread pan.

Sift dry ingredients together in a mixing bowl.
In another small bowl mix egg replacer and water until dissolved.
Stir in vanilla and vegetable oil. Add to dry ingredients and stir well until blended. Stir in the grated zucchini. Pour into baking pan. Bake one hour. Remove from oven and cool for 10 minutes, then turn onto a rack to finish cooling.

Cranberry Sauce

1 package fresh Cranberries
1 c Water
1 c Sugar

Wash and sort cranberries.

Bring water to a boil in a medium saucepan. Add sugar and stir until dissolved.

Add cranberries and stir until cranberries pop. Simmer for 10-12 minutes stirring often until sauce thickens.

Refrigerate until cool and firm.

White Sauce (or Vegan Bechamel Sauce)

2 T Vegan Margarine   ½ t Salt
2 T White Flour   1 c Soy Milk

Melt margarine in a double boiler. Add flour, and blend with a wire whisk or a wooden spoon, stirring until the mixture is smooth and bubbly (3 – 5 minutes). Slowly stir in soy milk, stirring constantly to avoid lumps. Cook and stir until the sauce thickens.

To make creamed soups, use the same method and ingredients, but increase the amount of milk to 2 c.

For a heavy sauce to use in soufflés, use the same method and ingredients, however increase the margarine and flour to 3 T each.

This basic white sauce makes creamed vegetable dishes very festive.

Mushroom Gravy

2 T Olive Oil

1 T Margarine

1 small finely grated Red Onion

2 T fresh Rosemary

½ t Salt

2 Cups warm Water

2 Cups chopped Shitake Mushrooms

¼ Cup Soy Sauce

2 ½ T Flour

½ Soy Milk

In a heavy skillet, heat olive oil and margarine on medium heat until margarine melts. Add onions and rosemary and sauté, stirring constantly until the onions turn brown. Stir in salt.

Add water and mushrooms. Simmer 15 minutes. Add soy sauce.
Quickly stir in flour and salt, add soy milk and simmer 10 minutes, stirring often.

Makes approximately 3 cups of gravy.

Desserts

Vegans diets are usually low in fat, high in fiber and healthy, just based on the ingredients that are used. But everyone likes to treat themselves to some utterly delicious sweets now and then.

The desserts in this section focus more on beauty and taste than they do on nutritional factors. They contain sugar and flour, but no eggs or dairy.

My grandsons have enjoyed baking together with me in the kitchen since they were three or four years old. We baked a layer cake and decorated it like a train for a fourth birthday.

Vegan Chocolate Cake

1 ½ t baking soda

1 t salt

½ c Soy Margarine

2 t Ener-G Egg Replacer

¼ c water

1 t vanilla

1 c Soy Milk

1 T Vinegar

1 2/3 c Flour

2/3 c Unsweetened Cocoa Powder

1 ½ c sugar (or equivalent sweetener)

½ c water

Preheat oven to 350 degrees. Oil and flour 2 cake pans (8")

Mix soy milk and vinegar in a cup. In a large bowl, stir together flour, cocoa, sugar, baking soda, and salt. Add margarine, vanilla, ½ c water, soy milk and vinegar mixture. Mix Ener-G Egg Replacer and ¼ c water until smooth and add to other ingredients in bowl. Beat with electric beater for 3 minutes at medium speed, scraping bowl frequently. Pour into floured pans.

Bake for 30 to 35 minutes, or until toothpick inserted in center of cake comes out clean. Remove from oven and let cool for 5 minutes. Remove from pans and cool on cake rack.

Vegan Chocolate Frosting #1

1 c Sweetened Cocoa Mix   ¼ t Salt

2 c sifted Confectioners' Sugar   1 t Vanilla

3/8 c Vegan Margarine   ¼ c Vanilla Soy Milk

With electric beaters, cream together cocoa mix, sugar, and margarine in a mixing bowl.
Add and beat until smooth: salt, vanilla, soy milk.
If the too thin, add more confectioners' sugar. If too thick, add more soy milk.
Makes approximately 1½ cups frosting.

Vegan Chocolate Frosting #2

1 c Powdered Cocoa (pure, unsweetened)   ¼ t Salt

2-1/3 c sifted Confectioners' Sugar   1 t Vanilla

3/8 c Vegan Margarine   1/3 c Vanilla Soy Milk

With electric beaters, cream together sugar and margarine in a mixing bowl.
Add and beat until smooth: cocoa, salt, vanilla, and soy milk.
If the too thin, add more confectioners' sugar. If too thick, add more soy milk.
Makes approximately 1-2/3 cups frosting.

Vegan Lemon Icing

3 c Powdered Sugar   1 or more T Soy Milk

3/8 c soft vegan Margarine   for Pink Icing

(Willow Run or Earth Balance)   (shown with Layer Cake), substitute

     Cranberry Juice for the Soy Milk

     Zest of 1 Lemon rind

Combine ingredients in a small mixing bowl. Beat with an electric mixer until smooth.

Vegan Layer Cake

2 1/8 c flour

1 ½ c sugar

1 T baking powder

1 T ENER G Egg Replacer

¼ c warm water

1/2 c vegan margarine (Willow Run or Earth Balance)

1 c soy milk

1 t vanilla extract or lemon extract

Preheat oven to 350 degrees.

Grease and flour 2 round 8" cake pans.

Sift flour, sugar, and baking powder into a large mixing bowl.

Mix Egg Replacer with water in a separate bowl until smooth.

Add mixture to dry ingredients and add vegan margarine, soy milk and extract.

Beat 4 minutes.

Pour into cake pans and bake for 35-40 minutes or until toothpick in center comes out clean.

Vegan Pie Crust

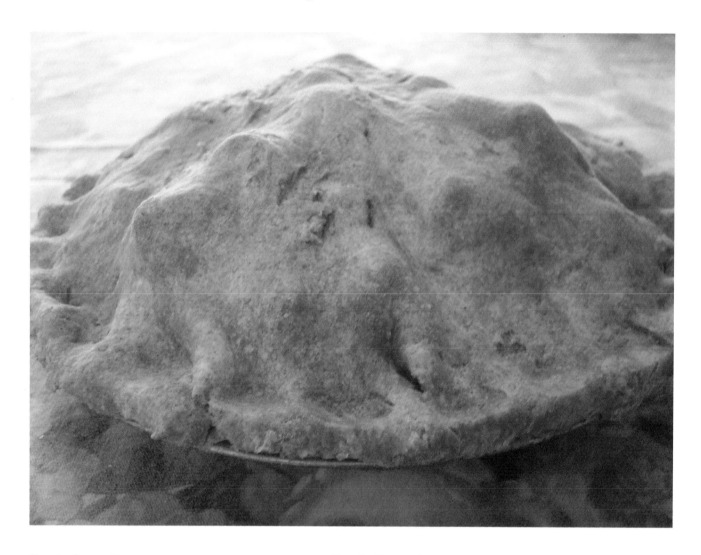

For 1 Crust Pie:
1 c Flour
½ t Salt
1/3 c + 1 T Crisco or Vegan Margarine
2 T Ice Water

For 2 Crust Pie:
2 c Flour
1 t Salt
2/3 c + 2 T Crisco or Vegan Margarine
¼ c Ice Water

Sift flour and salt into a bowl. Cut in Vegan margarine with a pastry blender until pieces are the size of peas. Sprinkle in ice water a little at a time, mixing with a fork. Form dough into a ball with your hands. Avoid over handling to keep dough cold to make the piecrust flaky. For a two-crust pie, divide the dough in half to form two balls. Flatten ball of dough onto a floured dishtowel. Roll with a floured rolling pin until less than ¼" thick. Roll until 1" larger all around than your pie pan.

For bottom crust:

Place the pie pan upside down on the dough. Carefully lift the edges of the dish towel while holding the pie pan and quickly turn upside down so that pie pan is right side up. Ease the dough into the pie pan. For a one-crust pie, flute the edges with your fingers and trim off the extra crust with a knife.

For top crust:

Gently lift the dishtowel and quickly turn it upside down to place the crust on top of the pie. Adjust the piecrust gently if needed and press the edges together with the bottom crust. Trim off excess crust with a knife.

Strawberry Pie

Bottom Pie Crust (Vegan)

1 Quart Fresh Strawberries

1 cup Water

1 cup Sugar

3 T cornstarch

Heat oven to 450 degrees F.

Prick bottom of pie crust with a fork several times. Bake crust for 12-15 minutes until golden brown. Cool.

Remove stems from strawberries, wash, sort and drain.

In medium saucepan, simmer 1 cup strawberries in 2/3 cup water for 3 minutes. In a bowl, blend cornstarch, sugar and 1/3 cup water. Stir into boiling strawberries and boil one minute, stirring constantly.

Arrange remaining strawberries in baked pie shell. Pour cooked mixture over strawberries. Refrigerate for 2 hours to cool.

Apple Cranberry Pie

Top and bottom pie crusts

1 c Water

1/3 c dried Cranberries

8 Apples

¾ c Sugar

1 t Cinnamon

½ t Nutmeg

1 ½ T vegan Margarine

Soak cranberries in water for 1 hour to soften. Drain.

Peel and slice apples.

Mix sugar, cinnamon and nutmeg together in a mixing bowl. Pour sugar mixture over apples, mix, add cranberries, and mix again.

Arrange fruit mixture in bottom pie crust and dot with margarine.

Add top pie crust and seal edges. Prick top with fork.

Bake at 425 for 50 minutes.

1/2 lb (2 sticks) Vegan Margarine, softened   1 3/4 c White Flour
1/2 c Confectioners' Sugar   ½ c Whole Wheat Flour
                                                1/4 t Salt

Preheat oven to 325 degrees F.

Blend the sugar into the margarine, then gradually add the flour and salt in a mixing bowl. Dough will be thick. Place the dough on a floured surface and roll out to ½ inch thick. Cut into squares or circles and place on un-greased cookie sheets and prick with fork. Bake for 25 minutes. Let stand 5 minutes. Remove and place on wire rack to cool. Store in an airtight container.

1 ½ t ENER-G Egg Replacer	2 T Flour
2 T warm Water	½ c Sugar
8 oz Tofutti vegan Cream Cheese	Grated Peel of 1 Lemon
2 T vegan Margarine	Juice of 1 Lemon
	2/3 c Soy Milk

Heat oven to 350 degrees F.

Thoroughly mix 1 ½ t ENER-G Egg Replacer with 2 T warm water. In a mixing bowl, cream the vegan cream cheese and margarine. Add sugar and egg replacer and mix well. Add flour, then add soy milk, mixing well. Add grated lemon peel and lemon juice. Pour into unbaked cracker crust. Bake 35 minutes. Chill well before serving. Garnish with fresh fruit.

Cracker Pie Crust

¾ package (18) Carr's Whole Wheat Crackers or Graham Crackers
1/3 c Sugar
½ c melted vegan Margarine

Place Crackers (18) in a plastic bag and crush with a rolling pin to make 1 ½ c crumbs. Melt margarine. In a mixing bowl, stir melted margarine and sugar into cracker crumbs. Press into bottom and sides of a 9" pie pan. Chill until set.

CPSIA information can be obtained
at www.ICGtesting.com
228832LV00006B